A Garden of Roses is Jesus

By Linda Singletary

Linda Singletary's books are available at special quantity discounts to use as premiums and sales promotions, or for use in training programs. To place a bulk order, please contact Linda Singletary at linda@lindasingletary.com.

ISBN-13: 978-1514268742

ISBN-10: 1514268744

Printed in the United States of America

Introduction

A Garden of Roses is Jesus! What a lovely thought! Back in 1942, Dr. Charles Weigle, the writer of the well-known song "No One Ever Cared for Me Like Jesus," also wrote a song entitled, "A Garden of Roses is Jesus."

Dr. Weigle told the story of while preaching a revival meeting in California, he walked through a rose garden on his way to church one evening. As he entered the building, people began to comment that he smelled like roses. Dr. Weigle realized that as he passed though the garden his clothing had picked up the scent of the roses, and that scent lingered with him.

This thought led him to write this beautiful song about how we can take on the fragrance of the Lord when we spend time in His presence. One verse of the song reads, "We may bring from the garden of roses sweetest fragrance from blossoms of love, from the presence of Jesus our Saviour, from the heart of the Father above."

These devotional lessons from the Song of Solomon are built on the idea of taking on the fragrance of our Lord. They will emphasize the importance of spending time in communion with Him--not just occasionally, but **every day**!

Have you communed with your Lord today? Is He a garden of roses to you?

Linda
2011

All scriptures are taken from the King James Bible.

Other books by this author:

Being a Contented Christian

Being a Fruitful Christian

Being a Teachable Christian

How About Your Heart?

It's a Jungle Out There

The Beauty of Holiness

Walk in the Spirit

Wanted! Godly Women

Table of Contents

Lesson One

"What's It All About?"

"What's It All About?"

"The song of songs, which is Solomon's." Song of Solomon 1:1

The Song of Solomon has never been one of my favorite books of the Bible, but since I have been reading through the Bible each year for many years, I have read this book many times. After reading the book this past year, I made a comment to my husband about how difficult I found the book to be. He agreed, and then told me that he had recently heard our dear friend, Brother Stan Blake, say that this was one of his favorite books in the Bible. I must admit that I wondered what was wrong with Brother Stan, but since I believe him to be a very spiritual man, I decided that I should investigate the book for myself to see just why it was one of his favorites.

I asked the Lord to give me understanding as I once again began to read the book—this time out loud. The second time through didn't seem much easier than the first, but I was reminded of Proverbs 2:4, *"If thou **seekest** her as silver, and **searchest** for her as for hid treasures; then shalt thou **understand** the fear of the LORD, and **find** the knowledge of God."* I really wanted to understand this book so I read it again and again, and this began my very interesting study of The Song of Solomon, which has resulted in the "hid treasures" of these devotional lessons. Notice, these lessons are not a commentary of the book, but rather devotional thoughts taken from the book.

The Author

Of course, God is the author of all of the Bible, but He used King Solomon to write this collection of love poems. (Song of Solomon 1:1) Because of its delicate subject matter, young Jewish men of olden times were not allowed to read the book until they reached thirty years of age. In reading the book, it is good to remember that God sanctioned married love and intended it to be a holy relationship. Hebrews 13:4, *"Marriage is honourable in all, and the bed undefiled."* Just as the tabernacle and the temple contained the Holy of Holies, into which only the high priest was allowed to enter, the Jews considered this book to be the Holy of Holies of the Scriptures—a very sacred book. While the book never mentions the name of God, His presence is very evident.

King Solomon, the wisest man that ever lived, was a prolific writer, and according to I Kings 4:32, he *"spake three thousand proverbs: and his songs were a thousand and five."* Evidently this song topped them all because Song of Solomon 1:1 calls it *"the song of songs."*

The Characters

While the commentaries sometimes differ about the characters in this book, I believe them to be King Solomon, the bridegroom; his young Shulamite bride; and the daughters of Jerusalem. Some writers believe the book was written by Solomon, but they believe the groom to be someone else.

The Setting

The setting of this book is in and around Solomon's palace in Jerusalem. Most of the scenes take place in the gardens, orchards and vineyards but some take place in the private chambers of the palace.

The Four Applications

There are four applications that can be taken from this book. (1) It shows the glory of wedded love; (2) in Old Testament days it was viewed as God's love for His chosen people, the Israelites; (3) it is a picture of Christ's love for His church; (4) it pictures Christ's communion with the individual believer. In these lessons we will explore this glorious communion that we as Christians can enjoy with our Saviour.

The Theme

This short book contains dialogue between King Solomon and his young bride. He expresses his love to her, and she to him. He describes her beauty and she describes his charm. While it is not always clear as to who is speaking in this book, I have come to the conclusion that is not nearly as important as what is being said.

These exchanges of love between the bride and the groom are given as examples of devotion for us as Christians to follow. Every Christian should take the time each day to get **alone** with the Lord. We need to talk to Him in prayer and then allow Him to speak to us through His Word. Our prayer time should not be limited to a prayer list; to just praying about our needs or even the needs of others. There should be time spent in fellowship with the Lord. While it is important to go to church and hear the preaching of God's Word, it is even more important to spend time **alone** with the Lord. It is always good to hear **about** our Lord, but how much better it is to hear **from** our Lord Himself.

One of the outstanding features of this book is that it speaks to the five senses—taste, smell, sight, hearing and touch.

- Song of Solomon 2:3, *"his fruit was sweet to my **taste**."*
- Song of Solomon 4:10, *"how much better is thy love than wine! and the **smell** of thine ointments than all spices!"*
- Song of Solomon 2:14, *"let me **see** thy countenance, let me **hear** thy voice; for sweet is thy voice, and thy countenance is comely."*
- Song of Solomon 2:6, *"His left hand is under my head, and his right hand doth **embrace** me."*

An Accepted Custom

Song of Solomon 1:6-7 tells us that Solomon's bride was a commoner who kept vineyards and tended to sheep. Still Solomon loved his young bride very much. I wonder in the beginning of their relationship if she even knew Solomon was King of Israel? No matter our status in life, the Saviour desires our fellowship. Song of Solomon 6:9 speaks of her as *"the choice one,"* who was praised by the other queens and concubines. What about those queens and concubines? The queens must have been the wives of Solomon, while the concubines were women living in the palace, belonging to him, but probably not known by him.

King Solomon is not only remembered for his great wisdom, but also for the many women in his life. I Kings 11:3 reveals that the King eventually had *"seven hundred wives, princesses, and three hundred concubines."* This book must have been written at an earlier time because Song of Solomon 6:8 mentions, *"threescore queens, and fourscore concubines, and virgins without number."*

A friend of mine who was born in China gave me some interesting insight into this custom. She said years ago in China, the emperor was entitled to have as many wives as he pleased. Many beautiful, young girls were brought to the palace and groomed to be presented to the emperor, but only a select few ever got to meet him, much less become his wife. If by chance one was fortunate enough to bear a child, especially a son, she gained rank.

Most young women never had this opportunity, however, and the sad thing was, once a girl was taken to the palace she was never permitted to leave. It definitely was not the glamorous life style it has often been pictured to be.

Though having numerous wives may have been the custom of the day, it was never God's plan for His people, and it was Solomon's love for many women that became his downfall. I Kings 11:4, *"For it came to pass, that when Solomon was old, that his wives turned away his heart after other gods: and his heart was not perfect with the LORD his God."* We must be careful to follow God's plan for our lives and not the accepted customs of the day.

In Song of Solomon 4:7 the bridegroom says, *"Thou art all fair, my love; there is no spot in thee."* This reminds me of a warning given in II Peter 3:14, *"Wherefore, beloved, seeing that ye look for such things, be diligent that ye may be found of him in peace, without spot, and blameless."*

As Christians, we have been made spotless, washed in the blood of the Lamb and covered by His robe of righteousness. We must be diligent to stay in close communion with Christ if we are to be found without spot when He returns.

Questions:

1. If we desire to understand God and His Word, Prov. 2:4 tells us to seek and search as if we were looking for _____.

2. Who was the human author of The Song of Solomon? _____

3. How many songs and proverbs did King Solomon write? _____

4. The Jews considered this book to be the _____ of the Scriptures.

5. Name the characters in this book. _____
   _____

6. List the four applications that can be made from this book.
   (a)_____
   (b)_____
   (c)_____
   (d)_____

7. List references to the five senses found in the book. _____
   _____   _____
   _____   _____

8. What turned Solomon's heart away from God? (I Kings 11:4) _____

9. What lesson are we to learn from this book? _____
   _____

Lesson Two

"Wake Up and Smell the Coffee!"

"Wake Up and Smell the Coffee!"

"I sleep, but my heart waketh: it is the voice of my beloved." Solomon 5:2

Some mornings I'm a real sleepy head so when I get up one of the first things I do is make a pot of coffee. Once in a while my husband, who doesn't even drink coffee, gets up first and makes the coffee. The wonderful smell of that coffee is a wake-up call for me, and it won't be long until I'll be out of bed and in the kitchen, enjoying a cup of coffee.

The Wake-up Call
Song of Solomon 5:1-6

The bridegroom speaks: *"I AM come into my garden, my sister, my spouse: I have gathered my myrrh with my spice; I have eaten my honeycomb with my honey; I have drunk my wine with my milk: eat, O friends; drink, yea, drink abundantly, O beloved."*

The bride speaks: *"I sleep, but my heart waketh: it is the voice of my beloved that knocketh, saying, Open to me, my sister, my love, my dove, my undefiled: for my head is filled with dew, and my locks with the drops of the night. I have put off my coat; how shall I put it on? I have washed my feet; how shall I defile them? My beloved put in his hand by the hole of the door, and my bowels were moved for him. I rose up to open to my beloved; and my hands dropped with myrrh, and my fingers with sweet smelling myrrh, upon the handles of the lock. I opened to my beloved; but my beloved had withdrawn himself, and was gone: my soul failed when he spake: I sought him, but I could not find him; I called him, but he gave me no answer."*

The groom was in his garden gathering spices. He must have found a bountiful harvest because he not only ate, but also called his friends to join him. It was still dark when he called to his bride, *"Open to me, my sister, my love, my dove, my undefiled."* She heard her beloved's tender words, but she had washed her feet and dressed for bed and had no desire to arise at this hour of the night. She was warm and comfortable and thought it better to wait until the sun came up and dried out the dew. But when the groom "put his hand by the hole of the door" and she smelled the sweet scents he had brought from the garden, she could no longer resist his call. She arose to open the door, but she had waited too long, and he was gone. She went out looking for him, calling his name, but he didn't answer.

In the book of Proverbs we read a warning about a similar situation. Proverbs 1:24-28, *"Because I have called, and ye refused; I have stretched out my hand, and no man regarded; But ye have set at nought all my counsel, and would none of my reproof: I also will laugh at your calamity; I will mock when your fear cometh; When your fear cometh......Then shall they call upon me, but I will not answer; they shall seek me early, but they shall not find me."* Our refusal to respond quickly to His call may result in His refusing to listen to us when we call on Him.

God wants to commune with us. He wants to answer our prayers. Proverbs 1:33, *"But whoso hearkeneth unto me shall dwell safely, and shall be quiet from fear of evil."* We are mistaken, however, to think we can come to God in our own time and on our own terms, and expect Him to bow to our every beck-and-call. Because the bride hesitated to answer the groom's knock, she missed the spices and honey in the garden, but more importantly, she missed some precious time with her beloved. When we are slow to answer God's call we are sure to miss both blessings and fellowship with our Lord.

I find morning the best time of day for me to fellowship with the Lord. I must come to Him before I get involved in other things or else I discover too quickly that the day is gone and I have not spent time with Him. Do you have a special time with the Lord each day, or are you too busy, or maybe, like the bride, just too lazy to spend time with Him? Spending time with the Lord may require sacrifice but the benefits are well worth the effort.

Revelation 3:10, *"Behold, I stand at the door, and knock: if any man hear my voice, and open the door, I will come in to him, and will sup with him, and he with me."* We often think of this verse as an invitation to salvation, but it is also a call for fellowship. The Lord wants to dine with us. Have you fed from His Word today?

Have You Answered These Calls?
The Call to Salvation: The Bible Speaks of several wake-up calls that we need to answer. The first is the call to salvation. I trust you have already responded to this call and have the assurance that your sins are forgiven and that you're on your way to heaven. Here are a few verses to help you if you have any doubts about this.

- Romans 3:23: *"For all have sinned, and come short of the glory of God."*
- John 3:16: *"For God so loved the world, that he gave his only begotten Son, that whosoever believeth in him shall not perish, but have everlasting life."*
- Romans 5:8: *"But God commendeth his love toward us, in that, while we were yet sinners, Christ died for us."*
- Romans 6:23: *"For the wages of sin is death; but the gift of God is eternal life through Jesus Christ our Lord."*
- Romans 10:13: *"For whosoever shall call upon the name of the Lord shall be saved."*
- Matthew 24:42: *"Watch therefore: for ye know not what hour your Lord doth come."*
- II Corinthians 6:2: *"Behold, now is the accepted time; behold, now is the day of salvation."*

Have you answered this call? Are you ready if He should come today? If not, don't put this decision off another day! Tomorrow could be too late!

The Call to Separation: Of course, salvation is just the beginning of the Christian life. The Lord has not only called us to salvation but He has called us to forsake our sins and live a life separated unto Him. If our lives are full of sin we cannot be of much use to the Lord.

- Romans 13:11-14, *"And that, knowing the time that now it is high time to awake out of sleep: for now is our salvation nearer than when we believed. The night is far spent, the day is at hand: let us therefore cast off the works of darkness, and let us put on the armour of light. Let us walk honestly, as in the day; not in rioting and drunkenness, not in chambering and wantonness, not in strife and envying. But put ye on the Lord Jesus Christ, and make not provision for the flesh, to fulfil the lusts thereof."*
- James 4:7-8, *"Submit yourselves therefore to God. Resist the devil, and he will flee from you. Draw nigh to God, and he will draw nigh to you. Cleanse your hands, ye sinners; and purify your hearts, ye double-minded."*

The Call to Service: When we know the Lord as our Savior we should make Him our Lord and be ready to share our knowledge with others.

- I Corinthians 15:34, *"Awake to righteousness, and sin not; for some have not the knowledge of God: I speak this to your shame."*
- Ephesians 5:14-16, *"Awake thou that sleepest, and arise from the dead, and Christ shall give thee light. See then that ye walk circumspectly, not as fools, but as wise, redeeming the time, because the days are evil."*
- John 4:35, *"Say not ye, There are four months, and then cometh harvest? Behold, I say unto you, "Lift up your eyes, and look on the fields; for they are white already to harvest."*

Love is the motivation for service. And without love service is nothing but drudgery. When there is love, service will produce joy. Psalm 100:1-2, *"Make a joyful noise unto the LORD, all ye lands. Serve the LORD with gladness: come before his presence with singing."*

Are You Listening for God's Call?

Solomon's bride heard his call but she was comfortable and didn't want to be disturbed. While she wanted to spend time with him, she was content in bed and not ready to get up. We, too, are often like this. We hear God speak, we agree with what He is saying and even intend to obey, but not right at the moment. We find ourselves satisfied with our lives and we don't want to get out of our comfort zone. We may be afraid we will fail, even though the Lord has promised to always be with us. Our failure to respond and step out in faith can cause us to miss out on God's blessings.

There are other times that we don't answer God's call. It may be because we're too busy, too preoccupied with ourselves, or that we are too distracted by the world. It could be because we are so cold and far away from the Lord that we don't even hear His call. What will it take to get our attention?

God Called Elijah in a Still Small Voice

In I Kings 19 we read how the Prophet Elijah stood with the prophets of Baal on Mount Carmel. The land was experiencing famine and they all prayed for rain, but Baal was defeated when God heard Elijah's prayer and sent an abundance of rain. Elijah's excitement didn't last long, however, because Queen Jezebel was angry and threatened his life, causing him to flee to the wilderness in discouragement. He sat under the juniper tree and prayed that he might die. We've probably all been under that juniper tree at some point in our lives.

God had other plans for Elijah and instead of allowing him to die, sent him food and renewed his strength to go on. Now Elijah had another problem. He felt he was the only one left who loved God. Still he did not forsake God, but rather waited upon God and strange things began to occur. First God sent a great wind, but He did not speak to Elijah in the wind. Next, God sent an earthquake yet He did not speak to Elijah in the earthquake. Then God sent a fire, but still Elijah did not hear from God. At last God spoke to Elijah in a *"still small voice,"* assuring him he was not alone and instructing him about Israel's future. Because Elijah was listening he heard the still small voice of God and then obeyed God's leading.

The Song of Solomon concludes with the bride saying to the groom in Song of Solomon 8:13, *"Thou that dwellest in the gardens, the companions hearken to thy voice: cause me to hear it."* If God were to speak to you today would you be able to hear Him? You, no doubt, could hear His voice in an earthquake, but what if He spoke in a still small voice? Today God speaks to us through His Word, the Bible. How long has it been since you allowed Him to speak to you through His Word?

Wake Up and Smell the Coffee!

Listen for the Still Small Voice!

Questions:

1. Where had the groom been when he called out to his bride in Song of Solomon 5:1? _____

2. Why was the bride slow to answer his call? _____
   _____

3. In Prov. 1:26 God said, "I will laugh at your calamity." Why did God say this?
   _____

4. Prov. 1:33 says, "But whoso hearkeneth unto me shall _____, and shall be _____."

5. What type of call is given in II Cor. 6:2? _____

6. Rom. 13:11-14 calls us to separate ourselves from sin. Verse 12 says "let us therefore cast off the _____,
   and let us put on the _____."

7. In I Cor. 15:34 God calls us to service. He says _____
   to _____ and sin not; for some have not the knowledge of God: I speak this to your
   _____."

8. How did God speak to Elijah in I Kings 19? _____

9. What was the bride's request in Song Of Solomon 8:13? _____
   _____

Lesson Three

"Take Time to Smell the Roses"

"Take Time to Smell the Roses"

"I AM the rose of Sharon," Song of Solomon 2:1

My favorite flower is the yellow rose. Roses have a fragrant smell, yet most of us live such busy lives we rarely take time to enjoy this sweet aroma. We may grow old before we have time for such simple pleasures, and by then find we've lost our sense of smell. All the advanced technologies and time saving devices we have today have failed to provide us with extra time. In fact, television, internet, cell phones, and many other electronic devices have actually robbed us of time.

Slow Down!

Activity is the mindset of the day. Even young children live very busy lives and get bored when they have a few minutes with nothing to do or no place to go. The little "Monster of Activity" appears so harmless, but he gets his foot in our door, gobbles up our time, and soon takes control of our lives. Christians are not exempt from this problem. We can be so busy **working for the Lord** that we have no time to **spend with the Lord**.

Stroll in the Garden of Prayer

Commune with the Lord: Much of the book of Song of Solomon takes place in the garden. Song of Solomon 6:2-3, *"My beloved is gone down into his garden, to the beds of spices, to feed in the gardens, and to gather lilies. I am my beloved's, and my beloved is mine: he feedeth among the lilies."* Hymns such as "In the Garden" and "Beautiful Garden of Prayer" depict the garden as the Christian's place of prayer and communion with the Lord.

Watch and Pray: Christ, Himself, prayed with His disciples in the garden of Gethsemane the very night He was betrayed by one of His own — Judas Iscariot. Three times the disciples fell asleep while their Master prayed and He admonished them saying in Mark 14:38, *"Watch ye and pray, lest ye enter into temptation. The spirit truly is ready, but the flesh is weak."* We, too, are weak and need prayer to keep us from the temptations of the world.

Many times our prayers are spoken while we're on the run, and while there's nothing wrong with that, there also needs to be those times when we get away from everything else and spend some quality time alone with the Lord.

In Song of Solomon 7:11-13 the bride calls out to her groom, *"Come, my beloved, let us go forth into the field; let us lodge in the villages. Let us get up early to the vineyards; let us see if the vine flourish, whether the tender grape appear, and the pomegranates bud forth: there will I give thee my loves. The mandrakes give a smell, and at our gates are all manner of pleasant fruits, new and old, which I have laid up for thee, O my beloved."* In chapter five the bride was slow to answer the groom's call because she was sleepy and didn't want to be aroused while it was still night. Now what a thrill it must have been for him to hear her calling, early in the morning, inviting him to spend time with her in the garden.

A stroll is a leisure walk—something we do for pleasure. When my family was here for Christmas we took several long walks which not only helped us burn a few calories, but also gave us an opportunity to talk. If I considered these walks and talks with my kids and grandkids so special, surely our Lord considers the time His children spend walking and talking with Him to be special. Slow down and make time in your busy schedule to stroll in the garden of prayer with your Savior.

Sit Under His Shadow

Song of Solomon 2:3, *"As the apple tree, among the trees of the wood, so is my beloved among the sons. I sat down under his shadow with great delight, and his fruit was sweet to my taste."* The bride, in speaking of her beloved, compares him to an apple tree, which she considers superior to the other trees. How she enjoys both his shade and his fruit.

A Place of Refreshment: I love the two apple trees in my backyard. In spring they are arrayed with fragrant blossoms; in summer they provide a shady place to relax, eat, and entertain guests; and in early fall they produce delicious fruit which we preserve in the freezer and enjoy all winter long. How I miss a third apple tree that was in our yard, but it died and had to be cut down. My hammock hung between two of those trees, and it was a wonderful place to read and meditate on God's Word as I watched the fluffy clouds float through the clear, turquoise, New Mexico sky. I called this my private resort.

A Place of Protection: We don't have to have an apple tree to fellowship with the Lord, but it does help to have a quiet place where we can get away from the cares of the world and concentrate on Him and His Word.

In this scripture the bride is comparing the apple tree to her groom. To sit under his shadow indicates she is close to him. This reminds me of other passages in the Bible which speak of our need to be in the shadow of His wings where He provides us protection. Psalm 17:8-9, *"Keep me as the apple of the eye, hide me under the shadow of thy wings, from the wicked that oppress me, from my deadly enemies, who compass me about."* Satan is out to defeat us, but if we stay under His shadow we will find protection from Satan's attacks.

Savor the Ointment of His Name

Song of Solomon 1:3, *"Because of the savour of thy good ointments thy name is as ointment poured forth, therefore do the virgins love thee."* Verse 14, *"My beloved is unto me as a cluster of camphire in the vineyards of Engedi."*

Many years ago some friends gave us a tin of Watkins Ointment. We never called it by its name, but rather we referred to it as Blake's salve because it was given to us by the Blakes. The label on the tin calls it Menthol Camphor and I believe camphire is another name for camphor. It has been on the market since 1868 and claims to be a pain relieving ointment as well as a medicated cough suppressant. It may not live up to its claims, but we always kept it on hand, used it for everything imaginable, and still use it today. It was sold only by individual distributors and last year, no longer knowing where to buy it, I went searching online. Finding an offer of free postage for ordering five tins, I got one for each of our three children, bringing back to them some childhood memories. When our grandson recently complained about chapped lips my son told him to use Blake's salve.

Just as our family proclaimed the merits of Watkins Ointment, the bride proclaimed the merits of her groom saying his name is like ointment which caused the other virgins to love him. Let's spend a little time **savoring the name of Jesus** and proclaiming His healing merits of salvation so that others may learn to love Him too.

Just as strolling in the garden means to leisurely walk; savoring His name means to deeply breathe or slowly taste. Many times I hurriedly read God's Word, but how much greater my delight when I slow down and meditate on it. Psalm 1:2, *"But his **delight** is in the law of the LORD; and in his law doth he **meditate** day and night."* Let's meditate on His name today!

The Names of Jesus: Isaiah 7:14, *"Therefore the Lord himself shall give you a sign; behold, a virgin shall conceive, and bear a son, and shall call his name **Immanuel**."*

Isaiah 9:6, *"For unto us a child is born, unto us a son is given: and the government shall be upon his shoulder: and his name shall be called **Wonderful, Counsellor, The mighty God, The everlasting Father, The Prince of Peace**."*

Matthew 1:21-23, *"And she shall bring forth a son, and thou shalt call his name **JESUS**: for he shall save his people from their sins. Now this was done, that it might be fulfilled which was spoken of the Lord by the prophet, saying, behold, a virgin shall be with child, and shall bring forth a son, and they shall call his name **Emmanuel**, which being interpreted is, God with us."*

Bless and Praise His Name: Psalm 145:1-2, *"I will extol thee, my God, O king; and will **bless thy name**, for ever and ever. Every day will I bless thee; and I will **praise thy name** for ever and ever."*

Psalm 148:13, *"Let them **praise the name of the LORD**: for his name alone is excellent, his glory is above the earth and heaven."*

Declare His Name: Hebrews 2:12, *"I will **declare thy name** unto my brethren, in the midst of the church will I sing praise unto thee."*

Glorify His Name: Psalm 86:12, *"I will praise thee, O Lord my God, with all my heart: and I will **glorify thy name** for evermore."*

Wait on His Name: Psalm 52:9, *"I will praise thee for ever, because thou hast done it: and I will **wait on thy name**; for it is good before thy saints."*

His Name Causes Controversy: No other name has ever been or will ever be as controversial as the name of Jesus. His name is the most loved and at the same time, the most hated name in all the earth. Why is there so much controversy over His name? If He were just an ordinary man His name would not be banned from public places, but **He is not an ordinary man. He is God, the Creator and Savior of the world**.

My daughter-in-law is a second grade teacher in a public school in Texas. Before Thanksgiving the children in her school were asked to write essays about being thankful. Each teacher was to select the best essay from her class and that child would then read his or her essay at an assembly program.

My daughter-in-law selected an essay by a boy in which the first paragraph gave praise to his Savior, Jesus Christ. Another teacher questioned whether he should be allowed to read this at the assembly, but the principal gave her approval for it to be read. However, when the boy got up to read his essay, he omitted the first paragraph. Asked why he had done this, he said he didn't think he would be allowed to mention Jesus's name. What a shame that the news media had put this kind of fear into a second grade child. In these days it is more important than ever before that we mention His name at every opportunity.

His Word is Magnified Above His Name: Psalm 138:2, *"I will worship toward thy holy temple, and praise thy name for thy loving kindness and for thy truth: for thou hast **magnified thy word above all thy name.**"* If we are to savor His name we must savor His Word!

At His Name Everyone Will Bow: Philippians 2:9-11, *"Wherefore God also hath highly exalted him, and given him a name, which is above every name. That at the **name of Jesus every knee should bow**, of things in heaven, and things in earth, and things under the earth; and that **every tongue should confess** that Jesus Christ is Lord, to the glory of God the Father."* Many people have not yet bowed at His name, but the day will come when **everyone** will both bow and confess that He is LORD!

In these busy days don't let the "monster of activity" rule your life. Slow down, stroll in the garden of prayer, sit under His shadow, and savor the ointment of His name.

Take Time to Smell the Roses!

Questions:

1. As Christians, we can be so busy working for the Lord that we have no time to
    _____.

2. Where does Song of Solomon 6:2 say the groom had gone? _____

3. Hymn writers have depicted the garden as the place of _____
    _____.

4. In Song of Solomon 2:3 what comparison does the bride make about her
    beloved? _____

5. Song of Solomon 1:3 reads, "Because of the _____ of thy good
    ointments thy _____is as ointment poured forth."

6. What does the word savor imply? _____
    Ps. 1:2

7. Isa. 7:14 says "Behold, a virgin shall conceive, and bear a son, and shall call his
    name_____.

8. According to Matt. 1:23, the name Emmanuel means? _____

9. List some other names for the Saviour given in Isa. 9:6. _____
    _____

10. At whose name shall every knee someday bow? (Phil. 2:10) _____

11. Why is the name of Jesus so controversial? _____
    _____

Lesson Four

"Thank God for the Promise of Springtime"

"Thank God for the Promise of Springtime"

"For, lo, the winter is past, the rain is over and gone." Song of Solomon 2:11

As I write these lessons it's January, not even one month into winter, but I'm ready for spring. I guess I'm a warm weather girl, but I do enjoy the beauty of snow for a short time. That's why living in New Mexico suits me. We have four seasons, but we have lots of sunshine and snow usually doesn't last very long.

For Christmas, my friend Anne, gave me a book, <u>An Ideals: Treasury of Christmas</u>, which has beautiful snow pictures, plus poems and stories of Christmases of yore. On these winter evenings as I sip my coffee by the fireplace, I have enjoyed reading these stories and have pictured myself spending Christmas in some of those settings. Romantic as that has been I'm actually glad I can close the book at night and awaken the next morning to sunshine. In fact, I'll be glad when I can awaken to the warmer days of spring, but in the meantime I'll be content with winter realizing it has its benefits.

The Benefits of Winter
One thing is certain—winter will come once every year. In some places it makes its appearance more noticeable than others, and in other places it's hardly noticed at all. On the calendar it arrives on December 22 and hangs around until March 20, but that, too, can vary quite a bit. Winter with its cold weather, ice and snow, represents the trials and hardships that are sure to come at different times in our lives. These winter seasons of life might come in the form of sickness, the loss of a job, a financial crisis, the death of a loved one, or just a period of discouragement. We may question why they come, but the Bible tells us in Job 37:13 that God sends winter for three reasons. *"He causeth it to come, whether **for correction, or for his land, or for mercy**."*

For Correction: Sometimes God sends these winter experiences into our lives to get our attention. He may send them as judgment for our sins or to correct us for our disobedient ways. We are often well aware that we are not right with the Lord and that our lives displease Him, but many times we do nothing to change our ways until He sends some wintertime correction to us.

Throughout the Old Testament we read about the judgment God sent to the Israelites when they disobeyed, but He was long-suffering and always forgave them when they repented. He will do the same for us today. When we are going through a trial we need to examine ourselves to see if God is trying to correct us.

For the Land: Not all wintertime experiences are for judgment and correction, however. Some are just for our good. Just as freezing temperatures kill off harmful insects, and north winds blow away last season's dying leaves, winter experiences can prepare us for a fresh start. When we look out on a new snowfall everything looks clean, pure, white and beautiful. Job 38:22 speaks of the *"treasures of the snow."* Snow gives moisture and adds nutrients to the land, and winter experiences can turn us to God's Word which offers spiritual moisture and nutrients to our lives.

The dormant period of winter gives the land a needed rest, and winter experiences may slow down our schedules and allow us to spend more time with the Lord. A busy life can be as barren as a winter landscape.

For Mercy: The same cold and snow which causes hardships also provides a lot of fun times, such as taking a walk in the snow, building a snowman, riding a snowmobile, ice-skating, skiing, sledding or just relaxing with a good book before a crackling fire. Some of the best times in life follow a terrible trial, because when we have no strength of our own we may look to the Lord and see that He is truly an all-sufficient God. Let those winter experiences be learning and growing experiences. Accept them! Even be thankful for them. God allowed them to come into your life and you can benefit from them.

If you live in a place with long, severe winters, nothing could be better than a vacation to Florida or Arizona right in the middle of winter. Although it's winter in those places, it's an entirely different thing than winter in the North. People living in hot climates are even happy for winter to bring a reprieve from the severe heat of summertime.

The Blessings of Spring
Song of Solomon 2:10-13, *"My beloved spake, and said unto me, Rise up, my*

love, my fair one, and come away. For, lo, the winter is past, the rain is over and gone; the flowers appear on the earth; the time of the singing of birds is come, and the voice of the turtle is heard in our land; the fig tree putteth forth her green figs, and the vines with the tender grape give a good smell. Arise my love, my fair one, and come away."*

Spring Speaks of New Life: The groom called his bride to come away — to leave winter behind and enter with him into spring. He promised her beautiful flowers, singing birds, and fresh fruit. Spring is the time of new life. Snow and ice begin to melt and the frozen ground starts to thaw. Flowers push their heads up through the soil, bare trees sprout buds, and brown grass begins to turn green.

Salvation provides new life. We leave our past sins behind and embrace a new beginning. II Corinthians 5:17, *"Therefore if any man be in Christ, he is a new creature: old things are passed away; behold, all things are become new."*

Spring Reminds Us of Youth: Youth is the springtime of life. It is the molding and shaping time of life. Though wrinkles haven't yet formed, habits that will last a lifetime are being formed. Young people are normally full of energy and ready to try new things. Such happiness is displayed in the lovely sight of a bride and groom, and the promise their union will produce is like the first blossoms of spring. The ripple of a small child's laughter is much like the chirping of the springtime birds. Youth is a happy and active time of life.

Spring is a Time for Planting: Those of you still in the springtime of life must be sure to plant seeds of love, kindness and forgiveness for in years to come you will reap the benefits of what you sow. Galatians 6:7-8 says, *"Be not deceived; God is not mocked: for whatsoever a man soweth, that will he also reap. For he that soweth to his flesh shall of the flesh reap corruption; but he that soweth to the Spirit shall of his Spirit reap life everlasting."* Throughout life we must continue to sow God's Word in our hearts for that is what keeps us from sin. Psalm 119:11, *"Thy word have I hid in mine heart, that I might not sin against thee."*

Spring May be Unpredictable: Spring holds some unpredictable days, especially here in the mountains of New Mexico. One day may be sunny and warm and the next day the cold March winds blow. We sometimes have more snow in spring than we do in winter, but we appreciate the essential moisture it provides.

The Hope of Eternal Springtime

Song of Solomon 2:8-9, *"The voice of my beloved!* **Behold, he cometh** *leaping upon the mountains, skipping upon the hills. My beloved is like a roe or a young hart: behold, he standeth behind our wall, he looketh forth at the windows, shewing himself through the lattice."* As the bride looked out her window and watched her beloved skipping about on the hills, she no doubt longed to be out there with him. Then finally the day came when he called her to join him.

Our Lord has promised to one day remove us from this wicked world and all its troubles and take us to the eternal Springtime of heaven. At the present we see Him through the window of His Word but one day we will see Him face to face. I Corinthians 13:12, *"For now we see through a glass, darkly; but then* **face to face.***"*

I Thessalonians 4:16-17, *"For the Lord himself shall descend from heaven with a shout, with the voice of the archangel, and with the trump of God: and the dead in Christ shall rise first: Then we which are alive and remain shall be caught up together with them in the clouds, to* **meet the Lord in the air***: and so shall we ever be with the Lord."* I Corinthians 15:52, *"In a moment, in the twinkling of an eye, at the last trump: for the trumpet shall sound, and the dead shall be raised incorruptible, and* **we shall all be changed.***"*

Song of Solomon 8:14, *"***Make haste***, my beloved, and be thou like to a roe or to a young hart upon the mountains of spices."*

Revelation 22:20, *"He which testifieth these things saith, Surely I come quickly. Amen.* **Even so, come, Lord Jesus.***"*

Thank God for the Promise of Spring!

Winter

In the cold, cold, dead of winter,
When the snow is on the ground;
I can feel a warmth in knowing
That God's love is all around.
Then His Word becomes so precious,
And we fellowship in prayer;
For God doesn't sleep in winter;
He's awake, He always hears.

Wintertime is, oh, so barren;
Not a leaf upon the trees;
Yet, it seems when days are dreary,
I spend time upon my knees.
Just as snow adds needed nutrients
To the dry, hard, frozen ground;
My heart needs the Holy Spirit
To convict, cleanse and abound.

When I sit before the fire
With the ambers burning bright'
It's a special time for resting.
All my burdens take their flight.
I reflect upon the summer,
And the busy days of spring;
Then I thank God for the quiet
Solitude that winter brings.

If we did not have the winter,
And the wind and rain and snow;
Would we appreciate the springtime,
And the flowers as they grow?
We would surely take for granted
All the sun-filled summer days;
If we did not have the winter
With its unpredictable ways.

Questions:

1. What three reasons for winter are given in Job 37:13? _____
   _____

2. What do we learn about snow in Job 38:22? _____
   _____

3. Spring speaks of new life. II Cor. 5:17 reads, "Therefore if any man be in
   _____, he is a _____."

4. Spring is a time for planting. Gal. 6:7 says, "Whatsoever a man _____
   that shall he also _____."

5. What does Ps 119:11 say that we should sow in our heart? _____

6. I Cor. 13:12 says we will one day see "_____."

7. What two sounds will announce the Lord's return? (I Thess. 4:16)
   _____

8. How fast will His coming occur? (I Cor. 15:52) _____

9. What does the bride say to the groom in Song of Solomon 8:14?
   _____

10. Our prayer each day should be, "Even so, _____
    (Rev. 22:20)

Lesson Five

"Don't Neglect Your Vineyard?"

"Don't Neglect Your Vineyard"

"...but my own vineyard have I not kept." Song of Solomon 1:6

Vineyards played an important role in the book of Song of Solomon. King Solomon had his vineyards, the bride's family had their vineyards, and the bride had her own vineyard. Evidently the bride had spent so much time tending to her family's vineyards that she had no time left to take care of herself or her vineyard. She evidently was questioned by the daughters of Jerusalem about her suntanned condition, because she answered them in Song of Solomon 1:5-6, *"I am black, but comely, O ye daughters of Jerusalem, as the tents of Kedar, as the curtains of Solomon. Look not upon me, because I am black, because the sun hath looked upon me: my mother's children were angry with me; they made me the keeper of the vineyards; but mine own vineyard have I not kept."*

In these modern times people love suntanned bodies. They spend hours in the sun, and the latest fad is to go to a tanning parlor, but I don't believe a tanned body was fashionable in Old Testament days. The bride mentioned being as black as the tents of Kedar and the curtains of Solomon. The people in Kedar lived in tents that were made from black sheep and goats, and the curtains in the temple must have been black as well. The bride asks her friends not to judge her for her black skin and explains that she got that way from long hours of hard work in the vineyards.

This young woman seems also to be bothered by the fact that she was forced by her siblings to spend so much time working in the family vineyards, that she had no time left to tend to her own. I believe Christians today often face a similar situation. We get so busy tending to the needs of others that we neglect our own needs. I'm not speaking about our selfish desires, but rather of our spiritual needs.

Being a pastor's wife for so many years, there were times when I tried to meet the needs of so many people that I didn't have the needed time to replenish myself spiritually. If we are to provide spiritual sustenance to others we must first saturate ourselves in God's Word. To always give out and never take in only drains us, and causes us to become spiritually dry and parched.

It is good for us to be concerned about others. We should be willing to drive someone to the grocery store or the doctor's office. We should take time to listen to their problems and answer their questions. We should be a friend to as many as possible, but while doing all these things we should not neglect our own spiritual well-being.

Don't Neglect Your Bible

If we are to advise others we must have Biblical answers to offer them. It is never enough to give our opinion about something—we need to know what God's view of the matter is. Proverbs 22:20-21, *"Have not I written to thee excellent things in counsels and knowledge, that I might make thee know the certainty of the words of truth; that thou mightest answer the words of truth to them that send unto thee?"*

The only way we can have those answers is to spend time in God's Word every day. Many Christians think they know a lot about the Bible, yet they go days and sometimes weeks without opening their Bibles. While it is important to read the Bible every day, that is only the beginning. To really know God's Word requires study, not just occasionally, but regularly! II Timothy 2:15, *"Study to shew thyself approved unto God, a workman that needeth not to be ashamed, rightly dividing the word of truth."*

Don't Neglect Prayer

Prayer is the most vital thing to a Christian's life, yet it is also the most difficult. Most Christians find it easier to work than to pray. How many times do we self-confidently try to solve our problems by ourselves before we finally pray? If we expect to accomplish anything lasting for the Lord we must pray. John 15:5, *"…for without me ye can do nothing."*

The greatest thing we can do for others is to pray for them, yet we often tell people we'll pray for them and then forget to do so. The Apostle Paul started many churches, and later wrote epistles to those churches telling them he was praying for them. He wrote to the church in Colosse in Colossians 1:3, *"We give thanks to God and the Father of our Lord Jesus Christ, praying always for you."* As we minister to others, let's not forget to pray for them.

Don't Neglect Church Attendance

If we are to survive spiritually we must be fed spiritually. We go to church to be fed by our shepherd or pastor. Jeremiah 3:15, *"And I will give you pastors according to mine heart, which shall feed you with knowledge and understanding."*

Both Solomon and his bride owned sheep. The bride asked Solomon in Song of Solomon 1:7, *"Tell me, O thou whom my soul loveth, where thou feedest, where thou makest thy flock to rest at noon: for why should I be as one that turneth aside by the flocks of thy companions?"* She didn't want her sheep to be fed by a stranger, but by the one she loved and trusted. How often do Christians seek spiritual food in the wrong places? While there are a few good preachers on television, there are many false prophets that may lead you astray. Matthew 7:15, *"Beware of false prophets which come to you in sheep's clothing, but inwardly they are ravening wolves."*

The groom answers his bride in verse eight, *"If thou know not, O thou fairest among women, go thy way forth by the footsteps of the flock, and feed thy kids beside the shepherds' tents."* He advises her to follow his flock to his shepherds' tents. I believe the shepherds represent pastors and the tents represent the Word of God. It takes discernment to know which sheep are in Christ's flock and which shepherds are feeding the flock. We must always compare what the shepherd is saying to what the Bible says. Jesus said in John 10:27, *"My sheep hear my voice, and I know them, and they follow me."* We must make sure we are in a good church where both the shepherd and the sheep are following the Great Shepherd, Jesus Christ.

Don't Neglect Your Family

God established the family. He created Eve for Adam and gave them children, making them a family. If you are a wife and mother you have a very important job—caring for your family. Titus 2:3-5 tells older women to teach younger women to keep their homes, love and obey their **husbands** and love their **children**.

As Christian women, next to our relationship with the Lord is our relationship with our husbands. While raising children, many women neglect their husbands, and when the children are grown they find their husband a stranger. Spend time with you husband!

Our next most important relationship is that of our children. Love your kids and take time to talk to them. Love is not giving them everything they want, or even meeting all their physical needs. Love includes teaching and disciplining. Proverbs 22:6, *"Train up a child in the way he should go: and when he is old, he will not depart from it."* The greatest thing we can do for our children is to lead them to the Lord. Don't become so busy doing for others that you neglect to teach and train your own children.

Don't neglect your parents! Exodus 20:12, *"Honour thy father and thy mother: that thy days may be long upon the land which the LORD thy God giveth thee."* The Lord will bless our dedication to our parents. I thank the Lord that I was able to care for my mother in the last few years of her life. Women without the responsibility of a husband and children may have an even greater responsibility to their parents.

The Dangers of Neglect
To neglect our spiritual vineyard can result in a disastrous fall. The Bible warns us about this. II Peter 3:17, *"Ye therefore, beloved, seeing ye know these things before, beware lest ye also, being led away with the error of the wicked, **fall** from your own stedfastness."*

So often we hear of seemingly successful preachers falling into sin. Remember, preachers are just men—capable of the same sins everyone else is capable of. If they don't depend upon the Lord they can easily fall. While tending to the needs of others, pastors may over-extend themselves. Many times these talented men can accomplish great things in the flesh instead of relying upon the Lord. In building big churches, they may neglect their relationships with their wives and their marriages fall apart. In teaching other people's children, they have no time for their own and they go astray.

As Moses led the Israelites through the wilderness he was kept busy from morning until night dealing with the problems of his people. We read in Exodus 18:13-26 that Jethro, Moses' father-in-law, observed how busy Moses was and discerned the potential dangers of this situation. He said to Moses in verse eighteen, *"Thou wilt surely wear away, both thou, and this people that is with thee: for this thing is too heavy for thee; thou are not able to perform it thyself alone."*

Jethro then advised Moses that after teaching the people God's laws and leading them in the right direction, he should select able men that feared God to oversee the people. He said in verse 22, *"And let them judge the people at all seasons: and it shall be that every great matter they shall bring unto thee, but every small matter they shall judge: so shall it be easier for thyself, and they shall bear the burden with thee."* Moses took the advice of his father-in-law and found this to be a solution to his problem. One person can never handle everything alone.

Let's not be too quick to judge preachers who fall. Satan is out to destroy God's work and rejoices when they fall under their heavy loads. I've heard it said, "the bigger the man, the greater the fall." We need to pray for our pastor and other men of God that they might remain steadfast in the work of the Lord.

Search your heart. Have you been so busy tending everyone else's vineyard that you have neglected your own? If you have, it's time to make some changes!

Don't Neglect Your Vineyard!

Questions:

1. What caused the bride to neglect her vineyard? (Song of Solomon 1:6)
   _____

2. Prov. 22:20-21 gives a solution for being able to answer others. "Have not I written to thee excellent thing in _____ and _____, that I might make thee know the certainty of the words of truth."

3. What do you think these verses mean? _____
   _____

4. What is the best way we can help others? _____

5. When should we pray for others? (Col. 1:3) _____

6. According Jer. 3:15 what is the responsibility of a pastor? _____

7. A person who is in God's flock will do what? (John 10:27) _____

8. Titus 2:5 says that women are to be "_____."

9. As a married women, after your relationship with God comes your relationship with whom? _____

10. To love our children also means we "_____" our children. Prov. 22:6

11. Exo. 20:12 teaches us to "_____" our parents.

12. Why did Jethro advise Moses in Exo. 18 to get help? _____
    _____

Lesson Six

"Watch Out for Little Foxes"

"Watch Out for Little Foxes"

"Take us the foxes, the little foxes, that spoil the vines: for our vines have tender grapes." Song of Solomon 2:15

A few miles south of Albuquerque is a run-down vineyard that's for sale. This vineyard has been neglected for several years, and I doubt that any grapes grow on those vines. There's a lot of work involved in operating a vineyard. In our last lesson we learned about the bride's suntanned body which was a result of her long hours spent working in the vineyard. There are hours spent digging, pruning, watering, repairing fences and many more hours spent gathering the grapes. In a properly tended vineyard the vines will become heavy with grapes, but that can all change overnight if intruders get into the vineyard, trample the vines and steal the grapes.

A Big, Bad Wolf, or a Little Fox?

It was little foxes, not a big, bad wolf that spoiled Solomon's vineyard, and it will probably be little sins that damage our spiritual vineyards. We seem to have a way of categorizing sins. Just as everyone fears a big, bad wolf much more than a little fox, we seem to think some sins to be worse than other sins, but in God's sight, sin is sin. To break just one link in a chain will break the chain, so to be guilty of one sin is to be guilty of them all! James 2:10, *"For whosoever shall keep the whole law, and yet offend in one point, he is guilty of all."*

How Big is Big, and How Bad is Bad?

As Christians who have a desire to live for the Lord, we're not immune to any sin, big or small. Sometimes we're on the alert for the big sins and let our guard down on the little sins, but more than likely it'll be the little sins that cause us the most trouble.

According to the Bible there are sins that don't look so bad in men's eyes, yet they look quite different to God. We believe murder to be much worse than hatred, but what does God say? I John 3:15, *"Whosoever **hateth** his brother is a murderer: and ye know that no murderer hath eternal life abiding in him."*

Surely lust isn't as bad as adultery? Matthew 5:27-28 says, *"Ye have heard that it was said by them of old time, Thou shalt not commit adultery: but I say unto you, that whosoever **looketh** on a woman to **lust** after her hath committed adultery with her already in his heart."*

We consider robbery a big sin, but just what does God consider robbery? Malachi 3:8, *"Will a man rob God? Yet ye have robbed me. But ye say, Wherein have we robbed thee? **In tithes and offerings**."*

The eighth commandment given in Exodus 20:15 says, *"Thou shalt not steal."* While most of us would never steal something from a department store, would we cheat the boss by using our time unwisely? I recently saw on the news where an Albuquerque city worker checked into work every day and then went home again for several hours. He didn't seem to see anything wrong with getting paid for hours he wasn't working. The city didn't quite agree and neither does God agree with such behavior. Robbery, stealing and cheating all amount to the same thing — they all break a link in God's chain.

So many sins we consider to be "little foxes" are sins of the tongue. James 3:5-6, *"Even so the **tongue** is a **little member**.....But the tongue can no man tame; it is an **unruly evil, full of deadly poison**."* We can misuse our tongue in so many ways and think nothing of it. Do you consider some sins to be worse than others? Lying, slander, flattery, gossip, sharp words and boasting are all sins. We might judge them differently, but how does God see them? Look up these verses and see what the Bible has to say. Psalm 12:2-4; 101:5; Proverbs 12:22; 15:1; 16:28; 19:5; 25:9; 25:18; 27:2. We're all sometimes guilty of some of these sins.

Proverbs 13:3, *"He that openeth wide his lips shall have destruction."* How many times I have regretted words I have spoken, but once spoken the damage was done. Think before you speak. Don't let these "little foxes" destroy your vineyard!

Little Foxes Trample the Vine of Fellowship!

As Christians, we not only take care of the vineyard — we are also part of the vineyard. In John 15:5 Jesus says, *"I am the vine, ye are the **branches**: He that abideth in me, and I in him, the same bringeth forth much fruit."* If little foxes get into the vineyard and trample the vines the branches can be damaged and even severed. The same is true in the Christian life. Little sins can damage and sever our fellowship with the Lord.

Just as broken branches won't produce fruit, severed fellowship won't produce spiritual fruit. Be on guard! Don't allow little sins to break your fellowship with the Lord and keep you from producing spiritual fruit.

Little Foxes Ruin the Tender Fruit!
The goal of every Christian should be to produce a bountiful crop of the best fruit possible. John 15:8, *"Herein is my Father glorified, that ye bear* **much** *fruit."* Galatians 5:22-23 lists the fruit we should desire in our vineyard, *"But the fruit of the Spirit is love, joy, peace, longsuffering, gentleness, goodness, faith, meekness, temperance."* Colossians 1:10 says, *"That ye might walk worthy of the Lord unto all pleasing, being fruitful in every good work, and increasing in the knowledge of God."* When we abide in the vine and fellowship with the Lord we are walking worthy of the Lord and that will result in fruitfulness.

Fruit is tender, easily damaged, and must be handled with care. New converts are tender spiritual fruits that need to be handled with care and with prayer. We can protect these tender fruits by being a good testimony and setting a right example. Sins, no matter how small and insignificant, can ruin our testimony, spoil our soul winning efforts, and hinder our good works.

Little Foxes Need to be Kept Out!
Fences, lights and maybe even a potshot now and then, are methods sometimes used to keep little foxes out of vineyards, and if we expect to keep little sins out of our lives we must use some of these same methods. Build a strong fence of prayer around your life to keep out those intruders. Use God's Word as a beacon of light so those little sins won't go unnoticed. Memorize verses to aim at those persistent sins to help ward them off. Don't let those little foxes spoil your vineyard!

Nip It in the Bud!

We'll not be able to keep out every little sin, so what do we do when one slips in? When we realize we have sinned, no matter how small we might consider that sin to be, we should "nip it in the bud" by confessing that sin. I John 1:9, *"If we **confess our sins**, he is faithful and just to **forgive us our sins**, and to cleanse us from all unrighteousness."* The next thing is to forsake that sin. We can only do that as we seek God's help through prayer.

Don't forget! Just as it's the "little foxes" that sneak in unnoticed and damage the vineyard, it's the little sins that creep into our lives unnoticed that break our fellowship with the Lord, rob us of our fruitfulness, discourage and defeat us, and may even ruin our testimony for the Lord.

> **"Take us the foxes, the little foxes, that spoil the vines:**
> **for our vines have tender grapes."**
> **Song of Solomon 2:15**

Questions:

1. What application can be made from the "little foxes" found in Song of Solomon 2:15? _____

2. According to Jam. 2:10 if we break one point of the law it makes us guilty of how much? _____

3. When we hate our brother God sees that sin as equal to what? _____ (I John 3:15)

4. What two sins are mentioned as equal in Matt. 5:27-28? _____ and _____

5. God sees our failure to give tithes and offerings as what sin? _____ (Mal.3:5-8)

6. What little part of our body causes us a lot of trouble? (Jam. 3:5-8) _____

7. What sin of the tongue is mentioned in Ps. 12:2-4? _____

8. What sin is mentioned in Prov. 25:9? _____

9. In order to be fruitful Christians we must "_____." (John 15:4)

10. According to John 15:5, Christians are what in the vineyard? _____

11. Where do we find the fruit of the Spirit listed in the Bible? _____

12. What do we mean by "nip it in the bud?" _____ (I Jn. 1:9)

Lesson Seven

"His Banner of Love"

"His Banner of Love"

"He brought me to the banqueting house, and his banner over me was love."
Song of Solomon 2:4

The bride was elated! The king was not ashamed of her; not ashamed of her lowly position as a shepherdess and vine dresser; not even ashamed of her suntanned body. Not only had he sat with her under the apple tree (vs. 3), he now brought her to a banquet at the palace and displayed his banner over her for all to see.

His Banner

An Announcement: We often see a banner stretched across a street announcing an upcoming event. Solomon's banner of love may have announced the arrival of his bride to the marriage feast at the palace. Have you announced to your friends that you are a Christian?

An Identification: A banner can also be a flag used as a symbol of identification. Our country as well as our fifty states all have flags that identify who they are. Solomon's banner of love identified this young woman as belonging to him, and her acceptance of his invitation to the banquet indicated that she accepted this identification. Christ has extended His banner of love to the world and when we receive Him as our Savior we accept His identification.

Baptism, a banner of identification for the Christian, is one of the first banners that should be displayed following salvation. Baptism does not play a part in our salvation, but it identifies that we have received Christ as our Saviour and want to be obedient to Him. Acts 2:41, *"Then they that **gladly** received his word were baptized."*

A Conquest: The flag flying over troops on their way to battle is a symbol of conquest.   Let there be no mistake about who they are, and that their purpose is to win the battle. When we join God's army we can be sure there will be battles ahead. We will never be able to win those battles in our own strength. Psalm 71:16 says, *"I will go in the strength of the Lord God."* To be victorious we must arm ourselves by putting on the armor of God every day. (Ephesians 6:11-17)

A Protection: A banner can also be a emblem of protection. Proverbs 21:31, *"The horse is prepared against the day of battle: but safety is of the LORD."* When we make Christ Lord of our life, He covers us with His banner. Psalm 140:7, *"O God the Lord, the strength of my salvation, thou hast covered my head in the day of battle."*

His Love

Better Than Wine: Throughout the book of Song of Solomon we see the love displayed between the bride and the groom. In chapter one verse two she says to him, *"thy love is better than wine,"* and in chapter four verse *ten* he says the same thing to her. While I've never tasted wine I do love grape juice, and I know this comparison of love to wine meant they both considered their love for each other to be exciting and wonderful.

In Bible days the word wine referred to any drink made from grapes. Let me insert a warning about the use of fermented wine or any kind of alcoholic beverages. As Christians, we have the liberty to drink wine, but to do so is unwise. Galatians 5:13, *"...use not liberty for an occasion to the flesh."* Proverbs 20:1, *"Wine is a mocker, strong drink is raging: and whosoever is deceived thereby is not wise."*

Our nation suffers today from the effects of alcohol. As a nation we seem to believe it's impossible to have a celebration without alcohol being served. We then wonder why drunk driving is such a problem. If you **never** take a drink, you'll **never** become an alcoholic, and you'll **never** be arrested for driving drunk.

God's love for us is even more exciting and wonderful than Solomon's love for his bride. Let's consider some ways that God's love is better than wine. One of the things people enjoy about wine, or any other strong drink, is that it temporarily causes them to forget their troubles. The problem is that when the wine wears off the troubles are still there, and many times they've been greatly multiplied.

God's love is eternal. Jeremiah 31:3, *"Yea, I have loved thee with an everlasting love; therefore with lovingkindness have I drawn thee."* Though God does not always take away our problems, His love will always be there to help us through our problems.

The bride says in chapter one verse two, *"we will remember thy love more than wine."* Memories associated with wine are not necessarily good memories, and wine may cause us to forget things we need to remember. Proverbs 31:4-5 says, *"it is not for kings to drink wine; nor for princes strong drink: lest they drink, and forget the law, and pervert the judgment of any of the afflicted."* On the other hand, our memories of God and His love are always good.

The consequences of drinking too much wine can be disastrous and even result in death, but God's love results in eternal life. John 3:16, *For God so loved the world, that he gave his only begotten Son, that whosoever believeth in him should not perish, but have everlasting life."*

Though we are undeserving of God's love, He loved us so much He sent His Son to die for us. Romans 5:8, *"But God commendeth his love toward us, in that, while we were yet sinners, Christ dies for us."*

Strong as Death: Song of Solomon 8:6-7, *"Set me as a seal upon thine heart, as a seal upon thine arm: for love is strong as death: jealousy is cruel as the grave: the coals thereof are coals of fire, which hath a most vehement flame. Many waters cannot quench love, neither can the floods drown it: if a man would give all the substance of his house for love, it would utterly be contemned."*

A seal is an official mark of authenticity. When we receive Christ as our Saviour we are sealed to Him for all eternity. Ephesians 1:13, *"In whom ye also trusted, after that ye heard the word of truth, the gospel of your salvation: in whom also after that ye believed, ye were **sealed** with that holy Spirit of promise."* John 3:33, *"He that hath received his testimony hath set to his seal that God is true."*

My marriage license bears the seal of the state of Ohio--the state where I got married. Many couples profess love and live as husband and wife, yet are not willing to seal their union with a marriage license. Can that be real love?

The Song of Solomon declares love to be a vehement or passionate flame that can't be put out, even by a flood. Nothing or no one can take God's love from us. Romans 8:35-39, *"Who can separate us from the love of Christ?..........For I am persuaded, that neither death, nor life, nor angels, not principalities, nor powers, nor things present, not things to come, nor height, nor depth, nor any other creature shall be able to separate us from the love of God, which is in Christ Jesus our Lord."*

Jealousy is sometimes confused with love, but love is never jealous. True love is **selfless**, while jealousy is **selfish**. I Corinthians 13:4-8 defines charity or biblical love. *"Charity suffereth long, and is kind; charity envieth not; charity vaunteth not itself, is not puffed up, doth not behave itself unseemly, seeketh not her own, is not easily provoked, thinketh no evil; rejoiceth not in iniquity, but rejoiceth in the truth; beareth all things, believeth all things, hopeth all things, endureth all things. Charity never faileth."* This is the kind of love God has for us. Is it the kind of love we have for Him and for others?

While loving and giving go hand in hand, giving alone is not love. Solomon says in verse seven, *"if a man would give all the substance of his house for love, it would utterly be contemned."* To contempt is to hate and the Bible often uses the word hatred as meaning to love something less. I believe this verse is saying that we could give everything we own and it would seem as hatred in comparison to genuine love. God gave the **ultimate** gift when He gave His Son as a sacrifice for sin.

We can never understand or explain God's love. Ephesians 3:19, *"And to know the love of Christ, which **passeth knowledge**, that we might be filled with all the fulness of God."* I John 4:8-16, *"**God is love**. In this was manifested the love of God toward us, because that God sent his only begotten Son into the world, that we might live through him...........And we have known and believed the love that God hath to us. **God is love**; and he that dwelleth in love dwelleth in God, and God in him."*

Questions:

1. List four things a banner might represent. _____
   _____

2. We identify ourselves as Christians by getting _____.
   (Acts 2:41)

3. Ps. 71:16 tells us to face spiritual battles in the "_____
   _____."

4. Song of Solomon compares love to what two things? "better than _____."
   (1:2) "strong as _____." (8:6)

5. Does a Christian have liberty to drink wine? _____
   (Gal. 5:13)

6. What verse in Proverbs says that to drink wine or other strong drink is not wise?
   _____

7. Jer. 31:3 tells us God's love is _____

8. Where do we find a biblical definition for love? _____

9. Rom. 8:35-39 lists ten things that cannot separate us from God's love. Name
   them. _____   _____
   _____   _____
   _____   _____
   _____   _____
   _____   _____

10. Eph. 3:19 says the love of Christ "passeth_____."

Lesson Eight

"Let's Talk About Jesus!"

"Let's Talk About Jesus"

"What is thy beloved more than another beloved, O thou fairest among women?" Song of Solomon 5:9

Tell Us About Your Beloved!

Have you ever noticed how a young woman in love never tires talking about the one she loves, and she will take advantage of every opportunity to sing his praises? It was evident to the daughters of Jerusalem that this Song of Solomon bride was in love. They questioned her as to why she considered her beloved superior to all the others, and this opened the door for her to tell them how wonderful he was. It should be evident to our friends that we love the Lord and our conversation about HIm should create a desire in them to know more about HIm. Of course, if we are going to talk about the Lord we must make sure that our lives measure up to our words. The old saying "actions speak louder than words" is very true.

I Peter 3:15 says, *"But sanctify the Lord God in your hearts: and be ready* **always** *to give an answer to every man that asketh you a reason of the hope that is in you with meekness and fear:"* Many people believe one religion to be as good as another, that all roads lead to heaven and that Jesus is no different than Mohammed or Buddha, but if this were true Jesus would not have risen from the grave. We need to have answers to give those with this kind of reasoning.

He is the Chiefest Among Ten Thousand: In Song of Solomon 5:10 the bride begins her description of her beloved by saying he is *"the chiefest among ten thousand."* I'm not sure if this young bride knew ten thousand other young men, but no matter how many she knew she believed Solomon to be the best of them all! The word chief means leader, ruler, highest in rank, the one of most importance. Her beloved was the one of most importance to her and she was declaring him her leader. Can others tell that Christ is important to you?

Christ should be the chief ruler in the life of every Christian. Colossians 1:18, *"And he is the* **head** *of the body, the church: who is the beginning, the firstborn from the dead; that in all things he might have the* **preeminence.***"*

Chief Cornerstone: Ephesians 2:20-21, *"Jesus Christ himself being the chief cornerstone; in whom all the building fitly framed together groweth unto an holy temple in the Lord."* Our lives and our homes must be built on Christ--the chief cornerstone. All other foundations are doomed to tumble.

Chief Shepherd: Just as Solomon was the **chief** to this young shepherd girl, Christ is **chief shepherd** to the Christian. In John 10:11 He is called the good shepherd, in Hebrews 13:20 the great shepherd and in I Peter 5:4 the chief shepherd. *"And when the **chief Shepherd** shall appear, ye shall receive a crown of glory that fadeth not away."* Praise the Lord, the chief shepherd can be my shepherd. (Psalm 23:1) We can know Him personally and be led by Him daily.

He is Altogether Lovely: In Song of Solomon 5:11-16 the bride continues her narration about her handsome groom. She knew him intimately, and enthusiastically described him, ending by saying, *"yea, his is altogether lovely."* Is Christ altogether lovely to you? How intimately do you know your Lord and how enthusiastically do you talk about Him? Isaiah 63:7, *"I will mention the lovingkindnesses of the LORD, and the praises of the LORD, according to all that the LORD hath bestowed on us."* Psalm 89:1, *"I will sing of the mercies of the LORD forever: with my mouth will I make known thy faithfulness to all generations."*

He is My Friend: The bride ends her discourse by saying in verse sixteen, *"This is my beloved, and this is my **friend**."* Now remember, this young woman was not King Solomon's only bride. He had many wives, yet to most of them he was not a friend, possibly to some not even an acquaintance.

Let's consider Queen Esther. Even though King Ashsuerus loved Esther above all the others, she still had to request to speak to him. (Esther 2:17) Because her request was granted she was able to save her people, the Jews, from destruction. I'm glad my husband is my friend and I can speak to him whenever I please.

Friendship is so vital to the marriage relationship. My advice to young women is to make a friend of the man you plan to marry before you marry him, and my advice to married women is to nurture that friendship so that it might grow stronger and endure the trials that may come to your marriage.

A friend is an intimate associate--someone we know very well. A friend is someone you can count on; someone who will be there when you have a need; someone who loves you in the bad times as well as the good times. Proverbs 17:17 says, *"A friend loveth at all times."* To have a friend requires being a friend. Proverbs 18:24, *"A man that hath friends must shew himself friendly: and there is a friend that sticketh closer than a brother."*

It was no doubt amazing to this young bride that she could claim the king of Israel as her friend. How much more amazing for us, as Christians, to claim the King of Glory as our friend. He is the dearest friend we could ever know. He is *"that friend that sticketh closer than a brother."* He knows all about us, yet He still loves us, and He is ready to listen when we call on Him.

He Is Mine and I Am His: Not only did this bride claim the king as her friend, she claimed to belong to him, and he to her. She spoke of this relationship three times in the book. *"My beloved is mine, and I am his."* (2:16) *"I am my beloved's, and my beloved us mine."* (6:3) *"I am my beloved's and his desire is toward me."* (7:10) While all of Solomon's wives belonged to him and were available whenever he wished, I don't believe he, in turn, belonged to all of them. It was quite an honor for this young bride to be able to say, *"my beloved is mine."* How wonderful it is for us as Christians to belong to the King of Kings. The incredible thing is that, we who are poor and unworthy, can say that He belongs to us.

Take Us to Your Beloved

The daughters of Jerusalem were so impressed with what the bride had to say about her beloved that in Song of Solomon 6:1 they asked a second question. *"Whither is thy beloved gone, O fairest among women? whither is thy beloved turned aside? that we may seek him with thee."* She had made him so appealing to them that they wanted to find him and see for themselves if what she had to say was true.

This young bride knew her beloved well. She had spent hours with him in the garden, and she didn't hesitate to tell them that he could be found there. Have you spent time   fellowshipping with your Lord in the garden of prayer? Do you know His Word so well that you could lead someone to the Saviour?

Blow Upon My Garden

In Song of Solomon 4:12-16 we read about the bride's fruitful garden, loaded with fruit trees and spices, plus fountains and streams of water. It was an enclosed garden, no doubt protected from those little foxes. There's just one problem. All of those wonderful fruits and spices that grew in that garden needed to be shared with others--not just locked up for her own enjoyment. In verse 16 the bride said, *"Awake, O north wind; and come, thou south; blow upon my garden, that the spices thereof may flow out."* She wanted the fragrance of the garden to waft out for others to share.

The north wind is usually thought of as cold and harsh, while we think of the south wind as being warmer and gentler. The gentle breezes of our lives may readily send forth the fragrance of the Lord, but when those winds of adversity blow will that same fragrance flow out? If we have spent time in His presence and taken on His fragrance, we will be able not only to endure those cold winds, but to be a fragrant breath of fresh air to those around us.

Let the fragrance of Christ radiate from me;
Pleasant aromas of love, joy and harmony!
May I savor His Word,
That my heart might be stirred;
And the fragrance of Christ radiate from me.

Questions:

1. I Pet. 3:15 says "_____ to give an answer to those that ask..."

2. Who is the head of the church? (Col. 1:18) _____

3. What is Christ called in Eph. 2:20? _____

4. Who is Christ likened to in I Pet. 5:4? _____

5. In Song of Solomon 5:16 the bride says "this is my beloved, and this is my
   _____."

6. Isa. 63:7, "I will _____ the lovingkindnesses of the LORD."

7. Ps. 89:1, "...I will _____thy faithfulness..."

8. Who is the friend that sticketh closer than a brother? _____

9. According to Prov. 18:24, what must we do if we want to have friends?
   _____

10. In Song of Solomon 6:1, why did the bride's friends ask where her beloved was? _____

11. What did the bride want to happen in Song Of Solomon 4:16?
    _____

Made in the USA
Coppell, TX
28 September 2022

83725315R10037